The last outpost of Europe before the rolling swell of the mighty Atlantic, Ireland is a land with a glorious landscape; a landscape shaped by the people who have lived there and by their way of life. But above all Ireland is a land shaped by the Celts. From the time that they first arrived, with their fiery tempers and artistic imagination, they have shaped the land to themselves. The constant warfare of the Irish chieftains and kings has left its mark in the ring forts and ruined towers dotting the scenery; buildings that recall the great heyday of Irish culture when chiefs led their warriors into battle and held court in huge halls to the sound of bardic harps.

Today, the Gaelic tradition is strongest in the west where the traditional rural life has been least disturbed. Here, too, the savage grandeur of the Atlantic coast is at its best. Throughout the long winter, storms lash the Connemara coast, throwing spray into the air and ringing the dark hills with a line of shining light. The great rollers that mercilessly pound the headlands and bays have been swept across the breadth of the ocean and release the pent-up energies of a thousand miles upon the wild shores of Galway. But in the summer, when gentle waves lap the shoreline, the treacherous rocks take on an air of limitless romance and enchantment. To the south of Connemara lies perhaps the most famous part of the Irish coast, Galway Bay. When the waters of the deep, broad inlet glitter in the evening sunlight and the sea birds wheel across the sky it is easy to see why this stretch of water has inspired the poetic genius of the Irish for generations.

Further south the Shannon spills into the ocean between Loop and Kerry Heads after a sluggish journey of some two hundred miles, fifty of which are along the tidal estuary. Beyond the Shannon Estuary the already scenic coast becomes truly spectacular as long fingers of rock push out into the blue ocean. The long inlets along this section of the coast are, in reality, sunken river valleys and the drowned contours can still be glimpsed. Perhaps the most beautiful of all these submerged valleys is Dingle Bay. The rich, verdant fields stretch across the land right to the edge of the cliffs that plunge down to the blue waters. Small, sandy bays are dominated by the rising mountains of County Kerry in the distance. Another of the bays, Bantry Bay, is famed far and wide as a deep water anchorage and can handle the largest oil tankers.

East of Kerry and its wild coastline lies the county of Cork. The southern coast shares much of the dramatic grandeur of the Atlantic coast, but is chiefly made up of charming bays beloved by holiday-makers. Off shore lies a string of islands famous for their wildlife and charm. Despite its more tranquil, peaceful air, this coast has seen its fair share of maritime disasters. In 1979, a yacht race from England around the Fastnet Rock ended in disaster when an unexpected storm sank many ships, and in 1917 the *Lusitania* was torpedoed off the Old Head of Kinsale. Upriver from Cobh, in the valley of the Lee, is the far-famed Blarney Castle. This great stronghold was built by McCarthy Laidir, who was descended from the kings of Munster, but it is not for its history that Blarney is known. Set high up in the wall of the keep, just below the battlements, is the Blarney Stone. It is rumoured that to kiss this stone bestows the 'gift-of-the-gab'.

The great scenic beauty of the west shoreline of Ireland is due to the strength of the rocks along its coast. It is these same rocks that form the beautiful, windswept mountains of Connaught and Munster. Stretching back from the coast are the uplands of the 'barren west'. The thin soils of the hills make them suitable for little except grazing and tourism. The hordes of visitors who come to the region in the summer for the scenery and the fishing bring an excitement and vitality to the area that has been lacking for centuries. In the Macgillicuddy's Reeks of Munster is the tallest mountain in Ireland, Carrantuohill, some three and a half thousand feet high. This line of high ground extends around most of the coast of Ireland giving a fine backdrop to the lovely coastal scenery.

Inland from the ring of mountains is a broad, undulating plateau of fertile land. It is here that the scenery reaches the typical view of the Emerald Isle and there are truly forty shades of green. Small crofts nestle amid the lush landscape where cattle and sheep are grazed and crops grown in abundance. It is as if the area is determined to make all the idealised pictures of Ireland come true. It is not only the soils and contours of the plateau that have created the landscape but the climate. Ireland's mild, wet climate is ideal for the crops and livestock that are so much a part of the scenery of the 'typical Ireland'.

Unlike the turbulent streams of the coastal mountains the rivers of the plateau are slow and sluggish, often becoming lakes or bogs along their courses. The Shannon flows from the slopes of Tiltinbane, County Cavan, through the whole of the central plateau to meet the sea at Limerick. Along its gentle path it flows through some of the loveliest land in Ireland and forms Loughs Derg and Ree. Loughs and bogs are among the great features of Irish landscape, spread across the face of the land. The bogs have their own part to play in the life of the nation. The peat they yield continues to be an important source of fuel for both home and industry.

From the mountains of Donegal to the valley of the Lee, Ireland is a truly beautiful country of green. Here the mind can drift back to days long gone; a time when life moved at a slower pace enfolded in the beauty of nature.

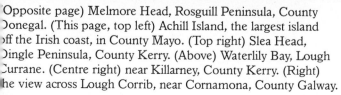

(Opposite page) Melmore Head, Rosguill Peninsula, County Donegal. (This page, top left) Achill Island, the largest island off the Irish coast, in County Mayo. (Top right) Slea Head, Dingle Peninsula, County Kerry. (Above) Waterlily Bay, Lough Currane. (Centre right) near Killarney, County Kerry. (Right) the view across Lough Corrib, near Cornamona, County Galway.

(This page, above) the city of Waterford, first settled by Norsemen in the mid-9th century. Reginald, son of Sigtryg, is reputed to have built the first church here, about 1050, where Christ Church now stands. The town's loyalty to the throne was demonstrated when the pretenders, Lambert Simnel and Perkin Warbeck, were refused admission. The latter, with the Earl of Desmond, laid siege to Waterford for twelve days without success. In reward, the city was given the right to the device *Intacta manet Waterfordia*. In 1649, it managed to repulse Cromwell's siege, too. (Top left and opposite page) stages in the making of world-famous Waterford crystal. (This page, top right) Muckross House, Killarney, County Kerry, where the skills of traditional weaving (centre right and right) may be seen.

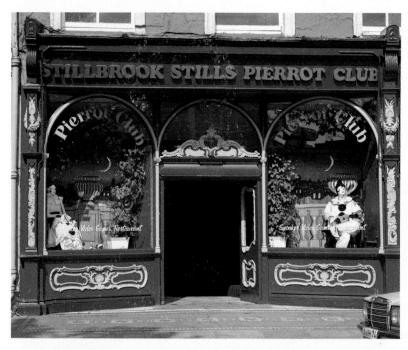
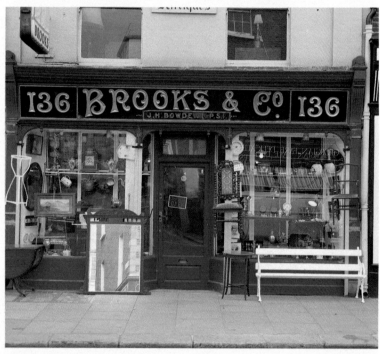

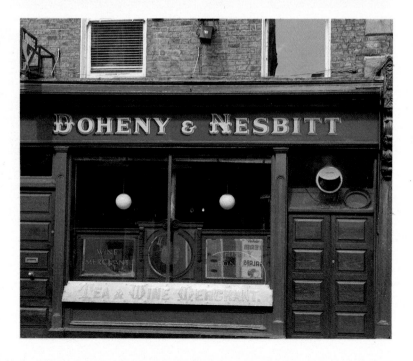

(Opposite page) colourful shopfronts line the streets of Dublin. (This page) the shoe department (left), food hall (above left and above right) and saddlery (top right) in Brown Thomas's on Grafton Street. (Top left and centre left) Greene's Bookshop on Clare Street. Dublin was known to Ptolemy who, in AD 140, marked it on a map as Eblana. Later, it was known as *Baile Átha Cliath*, the Town of the Hurdle Ford, by which it is known in Gaelic today. The site of the ford in its name is today spanned by Father Mathew Bridge. The blackish-looking waters of the Liffey as they reach the sea are responsible for the name of Dublin, for *Dubh Linn* means 'Dark Pool'. It was the Danes who developed the city as they found it a useful base for operations. Good Friday, 1014, saw their power destroyed by Brian Boru and his fierce Irish warriors at the Battle of Clontarf.

(These pages) in the pubs and clubs of Ireland is found the essential Irish love of song, laughter and a drink at the end of a hard working day. One of the popular kinds of drinking establishment is the singing pub, such as Hough's Pub (far left) in Banagher, County Offaly. The customers do the singing as they imbibe the traditional drinks of whiskey and stout. Irish whiskey, spelt correctly with an 'e', has a distinctive flavour not to be confused with Scotch whisky. The most famous stout in Ireland comes from the Dublin brewery in St James's Gate – Guinness – though it no longer arrives at pubs in wooden barrels but in metal kegs known affectionately as 'iron lungs'.

(These pages) the National Gallery of Ireland stands on the north side of Leinster Lawn. The building was designed by Francis Fowke and was opened in 1864. Housed within the same building is the National Portrait Gallery. The art gallery was originally financed by public subscription and, today, also receives one-third of the royalties accruing to the estate of George Bernard Shaw, whose statue (above left) by Paul Troubetzkoy stands by the entrance. Although there are naturally many examples from the Irish School, it is well known for its Dutch masters – including Rembrandt's *Rest on the Flight into Egypt* – and works of 17th-century Italian, French and Spanish Schools. There is also English work by Gainsborough and Hogarth. Work by Irish artists include landscapes by Nathaniel Hone and important portraits by John Butler Yeats. Several fine sculptures are displayed, too.

(Opposite page) Ballycopeland Windmill, County Down. (This page, left) St Patrick at Croagh Patrick, County Mayo, and notice to pilgrims (above). (Bottom left) Calvary statue, Healy Pass. (Below) Christ the King and Glen of Aherlow.

AR an láčair seo do šeas
an cíš inar Ruzaò
Diarmaid Ó Donnadáin Rosa
·Fínín aзus Tírzráčír·
·1831 - 1915·
On this site stood the house
wherein was born
Jeremiah O'Donovan Rossa
Fenian and Patriot
That brave and splendid Gael
unconquered and unconquerable
"Ní Déanfaiò Saell Dearmaò
orc зo bráč na breiče"

(These pages) Cork, whose name derives from *corcaigh*, meaning marsh. It was in the 7th century that St Finbarr founded a monastery on a small island within this swampy land. The Norsemen laid the foundation of today's city by making Cork one of their centres of trade. After the English, under Henry II, took the city from Dermot McCarthy the garrison were forced, 'to watch their gates hourly, to keep them shut at meals and from sun to sun nor to suffer any stranger to enter the city with his weapon'. (Far left) the *Innisfallen* in Cork Harbour. (Centre right) plaque commemorating O'Donovan Rossa.

(Opposite page) Kilkenny Castle. (This page, top) the Rock of Cashel. Here, in the 5th century, the King of Munster erected a *cashel* or stone fort. St Patrick preached there on the subject of the Trinity, explaining its nature by using the trefoil shamrock. The 13th-century cathedral was burnt in 1495 by Gerald, Earl of Kildare. He told Henry VII that he did it because he thought the Archbishop was inside! (Left) Galway's Salmon Weir Bridge. (Above) Dunguaire Castle, Kinvarra, County Galway.

(Opposite page) Adare Manor, County Limerick, was the seat of the Earl of Dunraven. (This page, left) Headford House. the magnificent estate of the Marquess of Headford. (Top) Bangor Castle, County Down, is an imitation English manor house which was built in the 1850s. (Below) Castletown House, County Kildare, is one of the finest Georgian houses in Ireland, and the headquarters of the Irish Georgian Society.

(This page, top left) near Partry, County Mayo, stands Ballintubber Abbey, known as the 'Abbey which Refused to Die'. Founded by Cathal O'Conor, King of Connaught, for Austin canons in 1216, it has been in continuous use for over 750 years. It had to be largely rebuilt after it was swept by fire in 1270 and has recently been renovated. (Above) Dunluce Castle, County Antrim, lies three miles from Portrush. The site has revealed evidence of early Christian and Viking occupation. In 1588, guns from the Spanish Armada ship *Gerona*, wrecked on nearby rocks, were used by Sorley Boy MacDonnell to reinforce the castle's defences. (Bottom left) close to the Rock of Cashel, County Tipperary, is Hore Abbey which was built by the Cistercians. (Left, below right and opposite page) Clonmacnoise, County Offaly. *Cluain Mhic Nóis*, The Meadow of the Son of Nós, is where a monastery was founded in AD 547 by St Ciarán. He had been given the land by Diarmaid Mac Cerbhaill of the royal house of the Uí Néill, who helped him to build the first wooden church there and became High King soon afterwards. There are extensive remains here today including O'Rourke's Tower (opposite page), dating from AD 1124, and the 12th-century church of St Finghin (this page, below right) with its round tower.

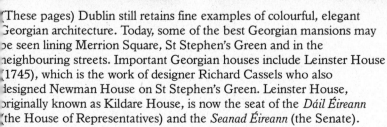

(These pages) Dublin still retains fine examples of colourful, elegant Georgian architecture. Today, some of the best Georgian mansions may be seen lining Merrion Square, St Stephen's Green and in the neighbouring streets. Important Georgian houses include Leinster House (1745), which is the work of designer Richard Cassels who also designed Newman House on St Stephen's Green. Leinster House, originally known as Kildare House, is now the seat of the *Dáil Éireann* (the House of Representatives) and the *Seanad Éireann* (the Senate).

(Opposite page) Dunbrody Abbey, County Wexford, was built about 1182. Because its charter gave the right of sanctuary, it also became known as St Mary of Refuge. (This page, above and top left) the Augustinian Abbey at Cong, County Mayo, was founded by Roderick O'Connor, the last King of Ireland. (Top right) the restored Cistercian Abbey at Holycross, County Tipperary, founded in 1169. (Centre right) Cahir Castle, County Tipperary. (Right) the Rock of Cashel, ancient seat of the kings of Munster. In the 18th century, the lead was taken off the Cathedral roof and sold by Archbishop Price.

(Left) University College, Cork, is situated on Western Road, to the west of St Fin Barre's Cathedral. It was founded in 1845 under the name of Queen's College, Victoria being the Queen in question. The fine building is made from carboniferous limestone and was erected on the site of 7th-century Gill Abbey. The library's collection includes some Ogham stones, Ogham being the early form of Irish writing. There are also several early, locally-printed books. In the grounds is the Honan Collegiate Chapel of 1915 with stained-glass windows by Harry Clarke and Sarah Purser. (Top and above) Ashford Castle, County Galway, is half a mile southwest of Cong, over the border in County Mayo. Built originally on the shores of Lough Corrib by the Oranmore and Browne family as a shooting lodge in the 18th century, it was later the home of Sir Benjamin Lee Guinness. He much improved the land and added to the size of the estate. On the western side of the castle may be seen the coat of arms of one of the members of the Guinness family; Lord Ardilaun. The property was bought in 1939 to become a luxury hotel.

(These pages) Ireland: land of sweeping hillsides dotted with sheep, tiny villages, quiet country lanes and a sense of peace which goes with a more leisurely pace of life. (Above) going to Belmullet's market, County Mayo. (Below) dry-stone walls march over the fields where the horse has not been supplanted.

(These pages) scenes in rural Ireland; spanning the rhythm of the seasons in a cycle that reaches back through the millennia. (Below) the scythe sweeps whispering through the tall grass and lays the swaths softly in sweet-smelling rows. (Bottom left) on the Muckross Estate, Killarney, County Kerry, may be seen a folk museum where the blacksmith shows his skill.

(Opposite page) Glenoe, from the Gaelic *Gleann Eo* meaning Yew Valley, is found in County Antrim. (This page, top left and left) the Sheeffry Hills near Delphi, County Mayo. (Top right) travelling in a jaunting car. (Above) a day out rock-climbing. (Centre left) young child and donkey, faithful friends in this land which lies wrapped in time's mist-laden kingdom, held golden in the hearts and memories of those that have left its shores, a country of verdant green; beloved Ireland.

(Opposite page) Tollymore Forest Park, County Down. (This page, above) near Moll's Gap, County Kerry, and the Owenreagh River (left). (Below) Lough Key Forest Park.

Storm gives way to sun, and rainbows – Nature's kaleidoscopic brushwork – sweep across the sky. (Left) St Mary's Cathedral, Killarney, County Kerry, is a Gothic-Revival church dating from 1842-1855 and designed by A.W. Pugin. It was renovated in the early 1970s at a cost of £278,500 when damaged plasterwork was removed to reveal the natural stone beneath. (Above) Father Mathew Memorial Church (1832) and Parliament Bridge (1806) in Cork. The church, with its soaring, graceful lantern spire, was designed by George Richard Pain and was the church of the Capuchin convent where Father Theobald Mathew – the 'apostle of Temperance' – was the Superior.

(These pages) land of raging torrents, foaming cataracts, and bournes the colour of whiskey as they flow over the rocks beneath. As the sun's light touches the river's relentless downward path (top left) it freezes for a moment in time the maelstrom of the waters. (Opposite page) the Owenriff River. (This page, top left) cascades on the Owenreagh River below Moll's Gap, County Kerry. (Top right) Aasleagh Falls, near Leenane, County Galway. (Above) Glencar Lake, County Leitrim. (Right) Ballynahinch, County Galway.

(Opposite page and this page, above) Mount Usher Gardens planted by the Walpole family. (Top and right) the Japanese Gardens at Tully House, Kildare. Lord Wavertree employed forty gardeners from Japan to produce this masterpiece. Wending through the gardens is the 'Path of Life', symbolic of man and the stages of his time on earth.

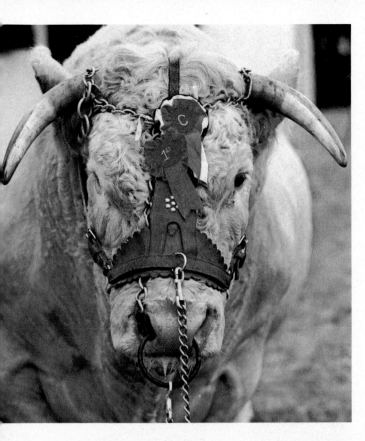

(Opposite page and this page, far left) the Dublin Spring Show. (Remaining pictures) an exciting day out at the Galway Races.

(These pages) Dublin Castle. (This page, far left) the main staircase in the State Apartments. (Left) the Portrait Gallery. (Below) the Drawing Room of the State Apartments with its magnificent chandeliers. The castle has been much altered since it was first commenced in 1204 by Myler FitzHenry, grandson of Henry I. The main entrance is at Cork Hill where, on the old main gate, the heads of Irish chieftains who defied English rule were displayed on spikes. The Bermingham Tower, which dates from 1411, used to be the State Prison and from it, in the 16th century, Red Hugh O'Donnell managed to escape to lead revolt against the English forces. In 1534, the castle withstood siege by Thomas Fitzgerald. It was the official seat of the lords lieutenant until the Free State of 1922.

(These pages) the Irish have always been close to the sea in spirit. (Opposite page) Dunmore East is an angling resort at the mouth of Waterford Harbour. (This page, top left) Kinsale, County Cork, was occupied by the Spanish under the command of Don Juan d'Aguila in 1601 but Mountjoy forced them to surrender. (Above) Killybegs, a busy fishing port in County Donegal. (Left) fishing in County Galway. (Right) the *Saint Jude*, at Carna, County Galway.

(This page, below) in Kenmare, County Kerry, salmon hang racked ready to be smoked to satisfy the gourmet's palate. The town was founded in 1670 by Sir William Petty (1623-1687) and colonized by about 75 Englishmen. They managed to establish a fishery and ironworks but were regularly under attack. In 1688, they were assaulted by 3,000 men and had to flee in two vessels, 'packed like fish one upon the other'. They reached Bristol after a fortnight. (Remaining pictures) Killybegs has a fine harbour on a small inlet of Donegal Bay.

(Opposite page) the Grand Canal, to the south of the River Liffey. (This page, top left and left) Phoenix Park, Dublin. (Above) thatched cottage on the Kenmare Estate, Killarney, County Kerry. Leisure time spent angling (below left) and horse riding (below).

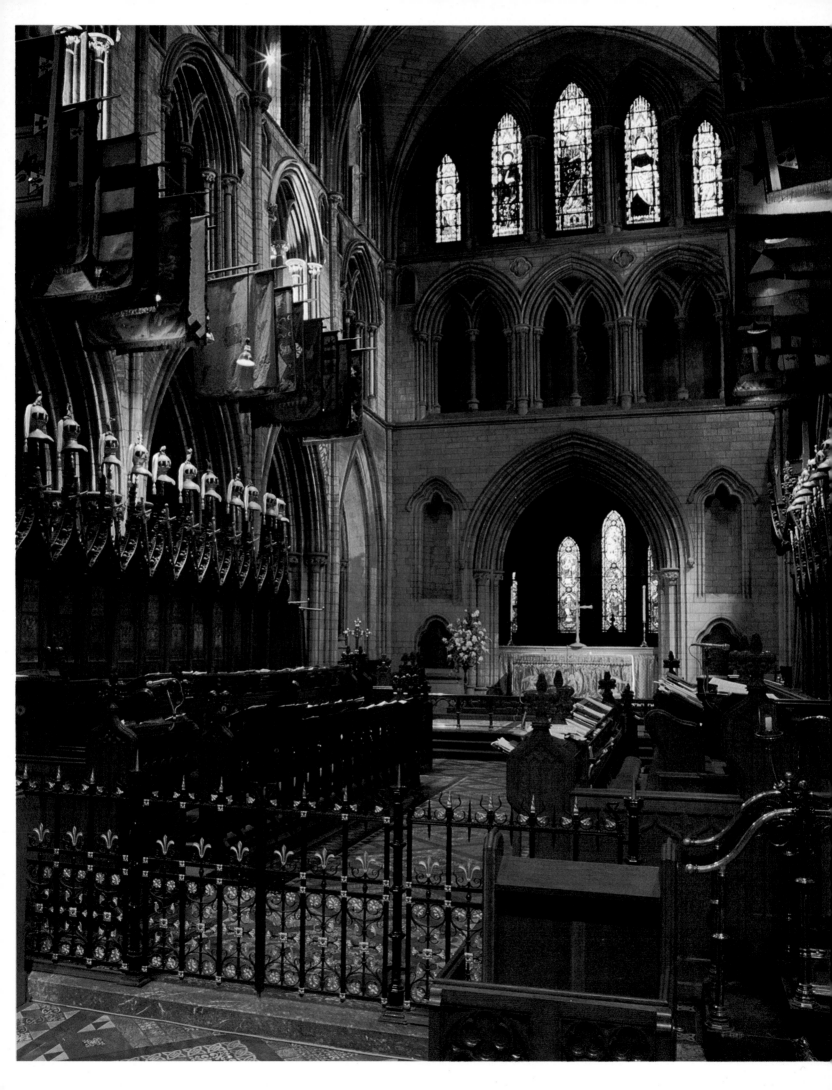

(Opposite page) St Patrick's Cathedral, Dublin, on the site of the Holy Well where the saint baptized converts. (This page, top) Franciscan Friary in County Wexford. (Above left) church interior in Cork. (Above right) inside the Church of Christ the King, Cork. (Right) stained-glass window in St Canice's Cathedral, Kilkenny.

(Opposite page and this page, top left) the National Museum, Dublin, houses some of the best examples of early Christian art to be found in Europe. Here may be seen the Feakle Treasure, found in 1948 in County Clare; many Bronze Age gold ornaments; the Ardagh Chalice, and the Cross of Cong which once held a fragment of the True Cross. (Far left and left) the 'Long Room' of Trinity College, Dublin. The flat plaster ceiling was replaced by the present barrel-shaped ceiling in 1856-1862. (Top and above) exhibits within the Rothgory Transport Museum in Dunleer, County Louth.

The hospitality to be found in the Emerald Isle is legendary. A warm welcome is assured to all who come to sample the fayre offered by the country's restaurants and hotels and the delectable delights contained within to please the tourist's tastes. (Opposite page) The King Sitric is one of Ireland's most attractive and successful seafood restaurants, being highly rated in the *Good Food Guide to Ireland.* (This page, left, far left and centre left) 'The English Market' in Cork. (Below, bottom left and bottom right) colourful Dublin Market and the shoppers who frequent its stalls.

(Opposite page) sunset over Glenbeigh on the Ring of Kerry. (Left) Clifden Bay, Connemara. (Above) view over Kingstown Bay from Sky Road, west of Clifden, County Galway. (Below) stormy sky at Slyne Head.

(Opposite page and this page, left) passing through the heart of Dublin is the River Liffey, stained a myriad shades of colour by setting sun or city lights. (Below) Bangor, County Down, is a famous seaside resort. St Comgall was born nearby, close to Black Head, and he founded his missionary abbey at Bangor about AD 555. He attracted many pupils and at one time had over 3,000 students. From these shores his evangelising disciples would set forth to preach the Gospel to the heathen Germanic tribes of central Europe. St Gall and St Columbanus were among those who went to convert them. Eventually, the fame of the monastery attracted the scourge of the land – the Norsemen – who destroyed all with fire and sword in AD 824. Several thousand died in that raid. About 1140, Abbot Malachy rebuilt the abbey. The Normans gave it to the Augustinians but the abbey was dissolved in 1542.

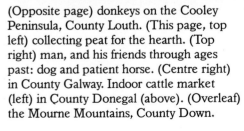

(Opposite page) donkeys on the Cooley Peninsula, County Louth. (This page, top left) collecting peat for the hearth. (Top right) man, and his friends through ages past: dog and patient horse. (Centre right) in County Galway. Indoor cattle market (left) in County Donegal (above). (Overleaf) the Mourne Mountains, County Down.